Contents

Introduction

PARENT PROBLEMS TWO - Looking Back at Our Parents' divorce
Young people's views on family life several years after parents have parted.

Bren Neale and Jennifer Flowerdew - *Centre for Research on Family, Kinship & Childhood, University of Leeds.*

This book, a companion volume and sequel to **Parent Problems**, adds a vital long- term dimension to our understanding of how young people cope in the aftermath of their parents' divorce or separation. **Parent Problems** provided us with a snapshot of the lives of these young people. This sequel will move beyond the snapshot to show what happens to these young people over time.

The authors followed up 60 of the young people who appeared in **Parent Problems** to find out how their lives had changed since they were first interviewed three to four years previously. This book presents first hand experiences from these young people on how they have sustained (or in some cases endured) their family lives over time, what has happened in their own lives and what strategies they have developed to help them manage.

A major theme of the book is what helps or hinders young people in moving on from the divorce of their parents to flourish both within and beyond their families. Some compelling insights are provided by them into the nature of their family and other relationships – in particular, how their relationships with parents and stepparents are played out, for good or bad, over time; how their relationships with friends and other kin feature in their lives, and how the nature of their family commitments may change over time as they move towards independence and think about the directions they wish their own lives to take.

Like 'Parent Problems!' this is a resource book for young people themselves. It will also be of interest to parents and to professionals working with families after divorce.

Chapter 1 Changing arrangements

Gabriella (8):

I feel it's up to me.

Rosie (13):

It's basically the same but it's got more flexible. It's not been as rigid.

Chaz (14):

If I see a bit less of dad at weekends. That's because of skating and seeing friends. It's nothing about dad.

Gabriella (8):

I spend equal time with mum and dad and I feel okay with that. I know it would be easier if they didn't live apart but I feel okay. I see dad Monday and Tuesday nights and then my dad's partner takes me to school on Wednesday. Then my mum picks me up from school Wednesday and we go to her. At weekends, we take turns with mum and dad. I think all that will continue even if it changes slightly. They always check it out with us. I feel it's up to me. Like I did say I wanted to spend more time with dad because I didn't think I was spending enough time with him. And they sorted something out. Sometimes they have little meetings and in these meetings they talk about what we want. Then they work out what they have to do.

Rosie (13):

It's basically the same but it's got more flexible. More because I've chosen. Like it's not been as rigid that I go to my dad's on certain days. I mean it's always been changed if one of my parents is busy, mostly my dad. But if there is something that I want to do, then (laugh) I'm the one who decides really. And sometimes, there are things that my dad is doing that I would be involved in, even though it's not on the right night. And if I want to go out on Sunday, then I go without my parents.

Sarah (12):

It's difficult. At one house, we are allowed to do one thing and at the other, we are allowed to do something totally different.

Clare (14):

It's 50/50, equal time with each. But cos my dad works late, if I'm at my dad's, I'll go to my mum's after school just to say 'hi' and drop in for a while. And then I'll go to my dad's. But when I'm at my mum's, if it's like a birthday during the week at anybody's house, then I'll just go there and spend a while there. They've talked about it to us and said 'Do you want to change it and spend like two weeks somewhere?' Cos it might feel like I'm swapping over too quickly and not getting settled in. But I think that would be just too long not to see each of them. At Christmas, one year I'll spend Christmas with my mum and New Year with my dad and the next year it will be the other way around. But my dad dropped in at my mum's on Christmas day. They didn't use to, but they've started getting on a bit better. So he drops in and has a glass of champagne.

Tom and Harold (12 and 15):

When they first divorced it was two days a week with dad. We saw him every day but slept over just a couple of nights. He lived nearby so we went to his house nearly every night. Mum would ring and I'd say 'Dad, can you come and pick me up?' And he'd just get in the car and pick us up and then he took us back. Sometimes, he picked us up from school and gave us our tea. Then things changed quite quick. Mum knew that we wanted to see dad more, so she let us sleep at his house three nights a week. And sometimes we stay more at dad's if mum's going out for a night. Dad just takes us. Or I might go round to my dad's house and we just wait there for my mum. It's quite important them living near each other because then you've got freedom. You can just go along whenever you want.

Frances (16):

I was about 8 and Lianne was about 6 when they first split up. My mum decided that we were going to have Tuesday and Saturdays at dads. But after a bit, we had some problems with my mum so we decided we wanted to swap it over. We asked mum. She wasn't happy about it and initially, there was a bit of a row with her about it (laughing). Then things got better with my mum so we decided that we wanted it half and half. Because it's fair, fair on everyone. We want to split the time half and half. We told dad and we told mum and then we worked it out a couple of years ago. It's better now.

Lianne (14):

It's exactly equal now. Monday to Wednesday morning I'm at my mum's, then Wednesday after school I come straight here to dad's, and I'm here until Friday. And then the weekends are alternate. It doesn't really matter what house I'm at as far as friends are concerned, I can still go and see them. Sometimes my mum and dad have got upset about having to go back and forth to get our stuff. Or sometimes, they've gone with my sister and forgot to tell me and I've been like 'Oh can I go to mum's?' and like it's 'Well, no, I've just been' (laughing). Sometimes I am a bit resentful but I prefer it much better this way than how it was before. I wanted it equal like it is now. I'm happy with it now but it's taken a very long time and lots of hard stuff in between.

Lyra (15):

I see my dad once a week. When I was younger I didn't stay the night but now I stay one night a week with him. It's the same with Magda, my mum's ex-partner, I stay with her one night a week too. I used to stay at dad's on a Friday. That's changed to Wednesdays because a couple of years ago I decided I wanted to start going out with friends and Friday night tends to be the night that people go out. But if I went out Friday night I wouldn't see him and I was only with him one day a week. There was no point me staying over at his on a Friday if I wasn't going to be there. But he is actually very good about all that. It is flexible.

Bobby (12):

Dad doesn't move around now so we're trying to see him like every two weekends. And cos I'm twelve and my brother's nine, we can just take the train there. We've got to know him more. We all made this decision - mum and dad and stepdad - that we could see our dad more often. Me and Don really wanted to see our dad a lot more often because of missing him.

Joseph (12):

It used to be something like one day a month with dad. Only one day and not the weekend. But my mum changed it to the weekend. And then I also have a week at half term and in the holidays. Now my dad rings me every Saturday and when he comes down to see me, he drives all the way. If I am just with him for a weekend, we stay in a hotel in the city, but if I've got the week, I travel up to stay with him. I've been doing that for years. I don't mind the travelling because I would rather see my dad.

Nina (15):

I still see dad but not as much. I probably used to see him every few days or something. I don't know, I can't remember. But now it's changed. We either see him once every few weeks or sometimes we don't see him for a few months. We don't really have an arrangement but we didn't really have an arrangement before. He just used to come round more often to see us. If we don't see him for a month, we usually phone him up and he says he will come round. Then we phone again and after a few reminders he will come round. I used to phone him quite a bit but I don't think I am really bothered any more. I was for a bit. I was disappointed that he didn't come round as much. But I began to realise that I wasn't really bothered about it when he actually did come round. I don't really feel comfortable with him. After I move out, I don't think I will see dad at all. I don't really have much of a connection with him. It's not like the relationship I have with my mum, which is not uncomfortable at all.

Charley (17):

I don't see my dad really now. Before, I was seeing him every second weekend. The last time I saw him was Christmas just for an hour so I'm not really comfortable at dad's. I think I feel in the way.

Karen (15):

Last time, I had three days at my Dad's house and four days with my Mum. But that has changed a bit now. I just spend two days with my Dad. I was feeling a bit that there wasn't much for me to do at Dad's. I don't have a computer at my Dad's and I use that for my work, so I thought I would have more to do here. And my dad was usually doing something else somewhere else, and I was usually just sitting around watching telly or something. I felt the situation was changing. I was actually quite depressed and it was getting to me a bit. I don't know, I just didn't feel like I was welcome to come in and invade his space and stuff. Dad didn't realize. I don't like to admit it but home is probably here at my Mum's really.

Sabrina (17):

Last time, when I was thirteen or fourteen, I was seeing dad like every Saturday and Wednesday. Then it sort of drifted off. I started to make excuses that I didn't want to be there. I couldn't be bothered. Some of my friends went out on Saturdays and I used to be at my dad's just sitting there. I was bored. My dad was just boring. We never used to go out and do anything. There was nothing. But at that age you want to do something else than just sit in the house. I didn't like his girlfriend either which didn't help. And recently I've just had so much work with college. And at a weekend I go out with my friends because everyone goes out on a weekend.

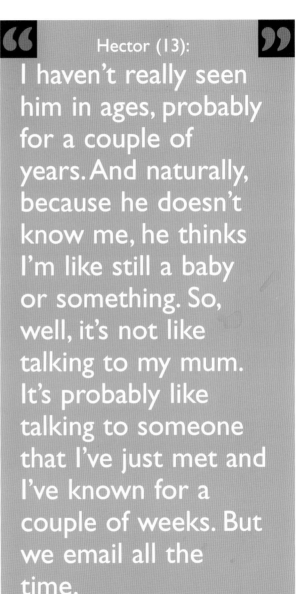

Hector (13):

"I haven't really seen him in ages, probably for a couple of years. And naturally, because he doesn't know me, he thinks I'm like still a baby or something. So, well, it's not like talking to my mum. It's probably like talking to someone that I've just met and I've known for a couple of weeks. But we email all the time.

Louise (17):

It like, really affected my dad when both his kids stopped talking to him because we both completely blanked him and everything. We didn't want anything to do with him for eighteen months. That was because he used to go every Friday and Saturday down to local club. And he used to just leave me, Jodie and John in the house. But well, time had gone past and I thought 'I'm fed up of this', you know what I mean. It's like I'm an adult now. I'm thinking 'Okay, you fell out with dad and it's never gonna be the same with him, but it's getting really stupid'.

Lisa (9):

I left my dad when I was not even a year old. I lived with him for less than a year. I only got in touch with him this year after 8 years. It was me who decided to get in touch. I wanted to know who my dad was. I've been nagging my mum for ages but she kept saying 'You're too young yet', 'You're too young yet'. Then one day when I was 8 I went 'Mum, can you find out who my dad is?' It was on my birthday when I went to see him. I asked my mum if I could have some time with him by myself and she said 'Yes'. And so I had some time by myself with my dad to ask questions and stuff. Like, 'How many relatives have I got?' My dad's got a huge family. He's got aunts, uncles and stuff. Loads of cousins. My dad, I love him a lot like my mum, because I've only just met him and he's not well.

Paul (11)

I never see my dad now. I used to see him a bit but I just didn't like him. First, he never took me anywhere or anything. Like he came and he bought me two things and that was it. And I wasn't that old then, about 8 or something. And he was grumpy. Like, if I was playing with my mate and he jumped off the bed with me and I tripped over or something and we were laughing, my dad would shout 'Right, Paul, bed'. And he'd say that he was right all the time so that's why I don't like him.

Joey (18):

I've been seeing dad slightly less because of my relationship with friends and because I was busy doing my A' levels and stuff. My relationship with dad hasn't deteriorated at all. It's just that he lives some distance away and my life here has become, not more important, but more involving. It wasn't an active decision. It just kind of happened. And dad does understand that I have a life here. It's not like I'm ignoring him or anything like that. I still speak to him frequently and when I go down there and see him at weekends, it's great. We go off and do stuff together like going to the theatre or out for a meal, that kind of thing. And that's really, really good. I never really do things like that with my mum 'cos she's like here all the time (laughs).

Chaz (14):

I stay every weekend at dad's, the Saturday and Sunday. I used to go about nine in the morning but now I go skating on Saturday, so it depends on what time we finish there. If we lived like very near him, I'd go and see him whenever, all the time. But like we moved here. When I'm older, get like to seventeen or something, I'll just go and see him during the week as well. When I've left school, I will go and see him more often, spend more time with him. Definitely.

When I'm older I'll just come to whichever house I want.

Jack (13):

Selina (20):

Coming to uni and having my own place was the nicest thing. For once I was settled. But when I go home, I still feel I have to split my time evenly.

YEAR PLANNER			
mum	DAD	mum	DAD
DAD	mum	DAD	mum
mum	DAD	mum	DAD
mum	mum	DAD	mum
DAD	mum	DAD	mum
DAD	mum	DAD	mum

Rachel (20):

I was reading some of the children's comments in the first book. Someone said moving between houses is like putting your life into carrier bags. And that's it exactly. You think 'yeah, I felt that'. I had this enormous bag that I would take back and forth from the age of about 7 (laughing) till I left home at 18. It's interesting to know that there are other people who have crazy schedules, who have to go back every third Tuesday for seven seconds and so on.

Jason (16):

Last time, I'd been seeing mum and dad 50/50. Then it changed a bit so that I was about a third of the time with my dad. That was a pretty long time ago now, probably about three years. Now I live completely with my mother. I hardly ever see my father. But that was my choice. I had been requesting that I got to live completely with my mum a long time before that.

Jack (13):

I've been doing a week with each one for as long as I can remember. When I was smaller I spent three days and then four days cos a week away from each one would have been too long. It will happen that when I'm older, probably like fifteen or sixteen, I'll just come to whichever house I want to come to. So if I'm over here, then I'll just come and sleep here, and if I'm like at my dad's I'll go and sleep there. It would depend where I was seeing friends and stuff. Because by then I'd be independent enough to just let myself in and out. As long as I told them where I was going to go, they'd be fine. If they didn't get on that would be more difficult. I mean dad comes round here and stuff and we spend Christmas together. They are friends.

James (15):

Mum wanted to see us as often as she could and my dad has always thought it was right to have 50/50. So they split it in half. They share us half the time. I mean I do actually feel sometimes that I'd rather live at my mum's house most of the time, but after spending my life seeing my dad, I wouldn't really want to just stop now. I'd feel really guilty and I wouldn't want to hurt anyone's feelings. In any case, if everything works out, I'll be leaving home in a few years anyway, so there's not much point. They both try as hard as they can but they end up having these arguments and stuff. Like if my mum hasn't got everything ready to take to my dad's house, he sometimes gets angry. I think he just likes being in control most of the time. And my mum ends up getting quite upset about it. I do think that if I could choose, if I had to choose which house I spend more time at, I think it would definitely be my mum's.

Claudia (16):

The actual 4 days at mum's and 3 days at dad's haven't changed. I might see dad a bit more because he's moved to where all my friends are. Mum doesn't like that at all. She can't understand that when I go over, it's to see my friends, not dad. She doesn't think I want to be with her, which isn't the case. It's got worse over the past year or so. Like I was supposed to be at mum's on Friday night but the way I saw it, Friday night was the one night that neither person kind of owned, cos they own our days (laughs). She'll say 'Friday night's my day', which pretty much says, 'I own Friday'. So last Friday I slept at dad's cos I'd been seeing friends nearby. The only way that I could get her to let me stop at dad's was to say that dad wasn't going to be in. 50/50 is fine. I just think that now I'm 16 I should have more of a say. I'll be moving out to university soon and then it'll be like, who are you spending time with each holiday (laughing)? Cos when you're at university you've actually got to decide for yourself. You'll have to actually say, 'ok I want to come and see you'. In a way it's easier now when they just agree it for us because then you don't tread on anyone's toes.

Selina (20):

Coming to uni and having my own place was the nicest thing. For once I had everything in one room. I actually felt like I was settled for the first time in ten years. Not living out of a bag. I lived out of four carrier bags for ten years. Before I came to uni, I had a week with one parent and then a week with the other. And in some ways I appreciate my parents more because I only saw them every other week. And I know it was hard for my parents too at five-o clock every Sunday, saying goodbye for a week. It wasn't easy for them either. It wasn't what they would have wanted but they had no other option really. But when I go home, if I go to mum's, I feel I'm upsetting dad. They don't try and make me feel guilty but I still feel I have to split my time evenly. And because I try to please everyone - mum, dad and friends - I end up pleasing no one. If I rush to dad's, he knows I'm rushing and he'll have a go at me: 'You just rush in and out and use this place like a hotel. You don't stay for any length of time and see me properly and nah, nah, nah, nah'. So then I have an argument with my dad and say 'For God's sake' and I just walk out. My mum is better, more understanding. But I've never been as happy as I have been in the past three years at uni. I'm settled. This is my home.

Angela (20):

There were times when I was at home that I wanted to change the arrangement but it just carried on. My Dad is a very dominant and strong personality. He is quite jealous so he gets upset if he doesn't have equal, or more than equal, of the time spent with my mother. He is a fiercely kind of, involved father. I remember a few years ago before coming to university. I met my fiancé and he came up and lived with me while I was still at home. So he went back and forth with me, which was mad really (laughing). Even now I've left home, I still have to try and balance it. Christmas is a nightmare. If I see Mum I have to see Dad. Even now, it is really ugh. I would recommend that the kids stay in one house and the parents move in and out. (laughing)..I think that's fairer

Chapter 3 Sorting out the money

It was a harder with money at first cos dad was working but mum wasn't.

Melanie (15):

Jason (16):
I think if you have a kid then you should support them.

Bobby (12):
When my dad and mum split up we didn't have much money at all. And we didn't really go to dad's cos dad didn't have much either. Things were much more difficult. We used to get cheaper clothes. We didn't live in as good house either as now. We kind of lived in a scruffy house and kind of, we just didn't get stuff we wanted as much. So like, if there was maybe a toy that we wanted, we'd have to wait like a couple of months, maybe half a year before we got it. So I kind of felt them splitting up was like a bit of a mistake. But things have got a lot better I reckon, a lot. Mum's got a better job now. And my step dad has a good job.

Fred (14):
I think my mum does worry a bit about money, because she's sort of got, well she doesn't have a set amount coming in. So she sometimes worries that she doesn't have enough.

Nina (15):
I think at first, when dad was giving us regular money, it was probably a bit easier for mum. He was meant to give us pocket money every week, and then mum paid for like keeping us and stuff. But then he couldn't pay it any more, and now mum gives it to us.

Emma (14):
It's hard for my Dad cos he lost his job a few months ago and couldn't afford to keep his car or come up to see us so often. But he comes up on the bus every fortnight to spend Saturdays with us. My step-dad also lost his job two years ago but Mum makes the best of it, changed where she shops and cut back on things.

Becky (16):
I've noticed that mum's buying us everything, you know, what we need and me dad is going on holiday. He used to pay for both of us but I'm sixteen now, so he doesn't have to pay for me. I mean he won't even buy me brother a new pair of shoes to go to school with, he'd rather spend his money on holidays.

> ## Louise (17):
>
> It was alright at first. My dad made sure my mum had the money for like me and Christopher and stuff. He'd never let my mum like be out of pocket. But about two years after they split up there were some problems with like child maintenance and stuff, and my mum hated my dad.

Daniel (16):

The CSA, the child support agency, they'd been involved but my dad appealed against it and won. I think he's a bastard not to pay anything. I think if you have a kid then you should support them. It makes me feel that there's no justice, especially considering that his job is to do with families and he can't actually have a decent family himself.

Sabrina (17):

It's been a bit naff to be honest. They used to argue about everything but now it's hardly ever, cos they never really speak to each other. Now they only argue over the money cos my dad won't pay any money towards us. I wish from the start dad would have paid maintenance. I think if he'd given a bit of money every week, everything would've been alright. We wouldn't have struggled the amount of times we did and they wouldn't have argued.

Hector (13):

My mum is reasonably quite well paid so that's no problem I don't think. Well we're not exactly, we're not exactly extravagant, but there's never been a problem about paying bills if you know what I mean...

Lyra (15):

I've got lots of friends whose parents have split up and it's horrendous because they just don't get on. Whereas my Mum and her ex-partner Magda, are best friends. Magda is always round here every night just for a cup of coffee. It's lovely. She gives my mum £100 per month or something for food and stuff.

Joey (18):

I think my family's great. I mean I'm sure there was stuff to sort out but they never, they never fought for possessions or anything like that. And dad gives money for us and has done ever since they were divorced. And I'm aware that it could, it could be a lot worse. I mean it could have been a really bad divorce. My parents could, you know, hate the sight of each other. You know, I'm just, I feel lucky.

Sarah (12):

They don't talk to each other about money and they don't argue about money. But they talk to us about money. Mum doesn't make dad feel bad about him having money, but she makes us feel bad. She doesn't do it on purpose but it gets to me. I feel guilty because I've got things off dad and mum hasn't got anything. And she thinks that we don't love her as much because she hasn't got as much money. And that's just not true.

Emily (14):

They just sort it out between themselves who pays for what. I don't even really like talking about it to be honest. That's strictly for them. I did get upset about it once. It was a little while ago. About my mum saying stuff like 'Make sure Sheila pays me for this'. All of a sudden I just thought, 'I don't want to know about your little money problems' and I got very upset. And so, yeah, they don't discuss money with us any more.

Rachel (20):

Whoever you live with, you have ups and downs with them. No matter whether they are your dad's partner or your dad's frog.

Elizabeth (12):

Quite a lot of people ask me if I like my stepmum or my stepdad better and I say 'Oh, don't ask me that'. I don't have a favourite. They're both really nice. I feel sorry for some people because they have horrible stepparents. And even though my brothers gang up on me and stuff and I don't get on well with my sister, it's fun having all these relatives.

Louise (17):
I wanted it to be like when I was younger, for dad to be on his own and be mine

Kevin (11):
Dad used to have a girlfriend called Ruth but they're not together any more. I didn't really like her. When I was speaking, she always used to interrupt me. She was just really annoying. Once when we were in the pub, I wanted to go home and I said to my dad 'Can we go home now?' And my dad said 'Just in a minute'. And she said 'I was about to say that Kevin's like a little kid. And then I remembered he is'. It was really weird.

Holly (13):

I think my main problem is that I've not met her. My dad has had other girlfriends but none has lived with us. And I've met them all as friends first, before my dad started going out with them. It's very weird and I think he doesn't realise how big it is, how much it involves. I think he thinks I'm going to be a bit down and a bit upset for a while, but that's it. I think it's going to be a bit more than that. And because we're going to have to move house, that's going to change the whole living near my mum thing. I'm sure I'll like her, it's not that. It's just a lot to expect of me to go 'that's okay'. It's just a bit full blown straightaway to get used to.

Becky (16):

I used to get on really well with my stepmum but soon as she got ring on her finger that were it, she changed. There were like four kids all of a sudden in the house. If you'd had more space, like somewhere to go when you wanted to be on your own, that would've been easier. And then, I used not to get on with my stepdad but I'd say that's got better.

Emily (14):

Up until last year, I thought my stepdad totally favoured his own children and was always horrible to me. But probably I was mistaken that he favoured them as much as I thought he did. I still have moments when I just can't stand him but that's the same with everybody really. I mean there's the odd moment when he tells me off instead of them when it wasn't me, but he does that with them as well. I'm very close to my stepmum because she sorts everything out. She's like a peacemaker. She's a social worker so she's really good with stuff like that. And my mum and her are like really good friends. They get on really well.

Sabrina (17):

Dad's got a new girlfriend and I get on with her and her kids. My dad's ex girlfriend used to slag our mum off to us so we were like 'No, you don't do that in front of us'. I didn't like that at all. But six months ago I went skiing with his new girlfriend and she was saying 'Well, I never slag your mum off because it's nothing to do with me and I've not heard both sides of the story'. I got on with her from then onwards really. It's made it a lot easier cos when I go round now I've got someone to talk to and dad won't start shouting at me in front of her. Mum's still got the same boyfriend. That's not a problem cos he's nice. We've known him for years and years. He doesn't really talk a lot. He's not in your face. He just moulds in. I'd hate it if my mum didn't have a boyfriend. She'd annoy me if she was round here all the time. It's nice that she can get a break from us by going over there.

Lyra (15):

I am very happy about dad's girlfriend. For me, the really strange thing is that she is a 'normal' woman. I'm sorry to use the word 'normal' (laughing). She wears lipstick and she likes clothes and she goes shopping. And mum and mum's partner are lesbian women. And then there's me, going out in my little poncy shoes and they just look at me and go 'ugh'. But then dad's girlfriend is like 'Oh I like your shoes' (laughing). And I enjoy that because it's different and I don't have that at all. I don't have that with mum either. She does understand my needs for clothes but with your mum it's different cos she's just your mum.

Bobby (12):

My dad has a new partner. It's good. She's nice and she's a lot like my dad which is good. And mum and my stepdad, they got married a year and a bit ago. My mum likes to make things big. My grandma and granddad wanted to pay for it so we had a really big party. We invited sixty people and it was really good. It was just really great. We had the ceremony in the afternoon with close friends and a party for everyone on the night.

Percy (14):

I'm close to my dad's girlfriend because she's like really nice and helpful and stuff. She sort of gets into things that we like, watches our television programmes and stuff like that. And she doesn't tell you off as much, or like punish you. She says how you get it wrong but then says how you got it right as well. And Steve, my stepdad got me into most of my sports like cricket and stuff. He plays cricket too, so he took me down and got me interested in that. And he's been really supportive if I've like got dropped from the cricket team. Or when I quit football club, he thought it was a good idea and stuff. And he's always ready to do things at the last minute. Like he'll come home and I've got to be out in half an hour and I haven't told him. But he's fine about it.

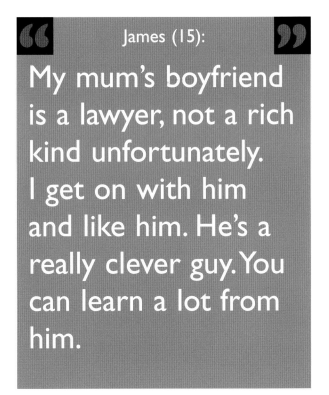

James (15):

My mum's boyfriend is a lawyer, not a rich kind unfortunately. I get on with him and like him. He's a really clever guy. You can learn a lot from him.

> ## Jason (age 16):
>
> Mum's got somebody who I call my stepdad but they're not actually married. That's about a year down the road, I think. I don't really like it (laughing). I mean I like Geoff but I just don't see my mum enough. He's a great bloke. He's just not as important as my mother. I want her to myself. She's mine (laughing).

Louise (17):

I used to get on with my stepmum but it changed. It was my dad. My dad were paying more attention to her then me and I didn't like it. I wanted my dad to pay attention to me and no one else. It was the fact that I was that age. I was being selfish. I wanted it to be like when I was younger, him to be on his own and be mine. But he never wanted that. He's always like wanted to grow old with somebody. I can understand that now I'm older. I was younger then but it's totally different now.

Cathy (15):

There was about six years between my parents' divorce and mum getting a boyfriend. And so, for that period of time, I'd got completely used to it just being the three of us. Me, my mum and sister. Now, even though it's two years on, I'm still getting used to it not being like that. And my dad has a girlfriend and she has children. It gets very complicated at times.

Joey (18):

"A year or two after mum and dad divorced, mum had a partner. That lasted for about six years so he did become quite a part of my life, him and his kids. They used to come here quite frequently, but after they split up they didn't come here very much any more. So I don't really see them any more. That was fairly sad, yeah. I think if they had lived round here, I probably would have seen them, stayed closer to them sort of thing. And I don't know why, but that didn't happen. Mum's now got a new partner. That's fine. I get on with him really well. He has a son of eleven but that's not difficult.

I don't feel challenged by him in any way. I suppose if they'd moved in just after mum and dad split up, or just after mum's first partner went, that might've been difficult."

Chapter 5. Difficulties in our lives

Ruby (13):

The divorce is *nothing*. It's everything *else*, one thing on top of another

Becky (16):

"I just hope that if I find someone, it doesn't go the way my mum and dad went and what happened to me and my brother. That if we have kids together, they don't feel like how I felt. I just felt disowned. I just felt so unhappy and nobody wanted me in their house."

Rachel (20):
You know, all parents mess up their children

Suzy (17):
Now I say to dad 'Excuse me, I'm not having that. I might be your daughter but I'm not being treated like that'.

Megan (14):
Things have just all moved too fast.

Leonie (15):
Anything I'd change? I'd change the way my mum is. It's like she won't talk to dad any more. She's just bitter. Basically it's the fact that my dad left her all those years ago and she still hasn't got over it.

Jason (16):

My dad knew that I wasn't sort of happy living with him. He must have done. It's probably three years since I changed it. It came about because I tried to run from my dad many, many times. He would try to keep me in my room to stop me from getting out. I moved out for many reasons but I'm not going to say what they are with a tape recorder on, that's for sure. My dad was blaming my mum completely, saying she was putting me against him. I heard he was very upset about me not going but at the time I wasn't bothered. Now I think my dad might have actually changed, his attitude to life might have changed, but I don't know, it's difficult to tell.

Alistair (15):

I've had so many problems with dad. He used to shout a lot. He still does a bit, not at me cos I would probably shout back, but sometimes at Helen. I mean it's understandable when it's something you've done wrong but sometimes it's just him in a bad mood. He used to be a bit violent but he's not any more. I'm bigger now and I know more than he does about some things, so it's kind of different. And I'm slightly more confident than I used to be. I don't know, it kind of changed when I spent less time with him. If I could change things, I suppose I'd change my dad, I think that's all (laughing). His anger, probably, controlling it, controlling himself really.

Helen (11):

Sometimes I wish that it could be a different life. If I look at somebody else's family, I would rather be in their place, cos I would love both the parents and not just mum. I realized, I found out about my dad. Before, I didn't really know, not like 'know' as in completely understand. Dad was not treating Alistair very well and I didn't really like going. I did ask Dad if I could see him less but he insisted that I stay there on Fridays. But now, I'm not seeing him any more. I didn't really make the choice until last Thursday. I had to tell him because I really didn't want to spend the weekend there. I couldn't. And even if he moved across the road from us, I wouldn't see him. The summer before last, Alistair decided he didn't want to see him again. So that made me kind of realize that I could leave whenever I wanted to. Allistair came back to dad's last winter. And I think dad's been much nicer to him now, 'cos he's worried. If I could change things, I would probably say that I wish I had never known my dad. Because then Alistair and I would never have to know what went on.

Sabrina (17):

My relationship with Dad has changed a lot really. I just didn't get on with him at all the last time. He got really nasty with me at one point. He used to take it out on me, no-one else. But no one believed me. He never actually hit me but he was just like throwing me around and stuff. And no-one ever saw that. And I used to tell my sister but she never believed me. But one time, when my sister was there, he did it to both of us, and she was just really scared. And I said 'Do you believe me now'? I didn't want to see him again for like ages. It's always been that I've been more sure in the whole thing about dad than the other kids. I have always been the one that sticks up for myself. And like now, if dad comes round and sort of puts me down, I'll say 'Excuse me, I'm not having that. I might be your daughter but I'm not being treated like that'.

> ## "Sometimes I wish that it could be a different life."
>
> **Helen (11):**

Joseph (12):

I did actually see a psychologist or whatever it's called for about two years. It was helpful, helped me to see things sort of in a different way. It was because I was like really angry with my step-granddad, my grandma's new husband, and I was getting so stressed. He is evil, he is really nasty. He made all the choices for my mum and he like helped split up my mum and dad really because he did a lot of mixing and stuff. Dad used to send me letters every week cos he was living so far away. But my step-granddad used to keep them from me and I didn't know my dad was trying to get in touch. It came out a couple of years later because my mum found all the letters. None of us like him.

Elizabeth (12):

Granddad dying. That was one of the main things that's happened since I talked to you last.

Nina (15):

Adam is a boy. He's my friend. He died in the summer holidays in a car crash. And just last Friday night, we had this big night for him in town. Cos he used to like going to techno and to raves and stuff. And it was like really buzzing. We had a 'one minute noise' for him and stuff like that.

Bobby (12):

When I was 6, Rick died. He was a really good friend and I had to go to a counsellor. That was helpful, because that was kind of my first dealing with death. I kind of had grief for a couple of years. I also had this nice teacher who died when I was eleven. I didn't really like school at that point but a few weeks ago I started High school. That's fantastic.

Elizabeth (12):

Well once when I got kind of really upset, I had to tell a teacher because they wanted to know what was wrong with me. And they were like really sympathetic and everything to me. That was about family stuff. Cos it was actually my cat, she died. She was really old, about twenty. I had to kind of go out of lessons and just wipe my eyes and stuff. And the teacher came and asked me what was wrong and I just told her.

Lauren (16):

School attempted to talk to me about family stuff but I was having none of it. I felt they were interfering. They had quite a few problems with me over various things I've done. And they thought it was about home because I hadn't been looking after my self for a while and they were like 'Do your mum and dad hit you?' and I was like 'No, there's nothing wrong at home'. I fell out with school big time over that.

Mary (17):

There's been a lot happening, but not so much in ways you'd be thinking about. Things are more or less the same at home. The big thing for me has been to do with my sexuality, coming out about it at college. It's been the most important thing for me over the past few years. I didn't dare say anything at school. It was only after my GCSEs when I left school and went to college that I felt it was okay to tell people.

Chelsea (13):

I have had a bit of stuff recently. Like all these children, the ones that think they're hard and stuff, somebody told them about my dad being gay. And so I had this stuff off them, just shouting it out or something. And I was like 'You should be ashamed'. And I could slap some of them but I don't because (laughing) it's like, it really annoys me, but it only happens occasionally. And I know, with all of them, they always have to have a problem with somebody. So it's like the next day, they'll move on to somebody else.

Lyra (15):

It is funny how when you get older, some things that didn't bother you before, bother you now. Like the lesbian thing, I know lots of people are prejudiced against lesbians and stuff. I used to be fine about it but now I sort of get a bit wary when we go to parent's evening and three people turn up, two women and a man. I feel a bit self-conscious. When I was like, I don't know eleven or twelve, I didn't think about it. I don't feel ashamed of them but all around me it is 'You faggot', 'you this', 'you gay whatever'. I am very aware of it in school especially. And I think, 'God if you knew my mum'. I imagine I will eventually say, 'Well stuff you, they are gay'. It doesn't affect me. I don't feel hurt about it because I have sort of picked up an immune system to it.

Ruby (13):

Every little bit just adds on an extra layer. Like Mum being with a woman. I don't know whether it makes it worse, but it's just something else you have to think about, another weight on.

Every little bit just adds on an extra layer.

Ruby (13):

Kerry (17):

I didn't believe it at first about Mum. Only our close friends know, cos if anyone else found out they'd be thinking 'like mother, like daughter' and we're not gay. But it's not the fact that's Sally's a woman, it's how she is. She has depression and we're sympathetic to that, but she's often in a mood. And we can't have friends round to the house any more whereas we did before. And when I was doing my GCSEs, things were all over the place and I did really bad. Dad had just finished with his other partner who was really nice. She had this really sweet little lad. We haven't seen them since cos his new partner doesn't like us to. So I made Dad help Ruby with her GCSE options.

Ruth (16):

Mum's partner wouldn't even say hello to me. I just felt like I wasn't there. This was when I was 7 or 8. She would just come in and sit with my Mum. And so, after that happened for a couple of years, I said 'Well I don't want to know you either'. And it hasn't got any better. I don't like what she is doing to my Mum. Because I understand she is depressed. I understand that. But my Mum has given so much and she has been there for her so much and it drains my Mum. You know, if you are with somebody who is depressed and you are with them loads, it really drains you, and it gets to you. And she doesn't give anything back and she is so self absorbed. She forgot to get my Mum a Christmas present. And I just get so cross with her.

Megan (14):

Things have just all moved too fast. When I was really little it was awful, them fighting and the police coming round. After a while Dad got a house and we could stay over, but just two nights a week. After that it got worse. I was taken to a family court, and asked what I wanted. I was 7, too young to think of a system. Then my Mum got ill so we started being with Dad more. My Mum didn't take that too well. It was a really hard time for a year or two. I was quite depressed. Other hard things happening were with the Child Support Agency. They took so much money off Dad that he nearly lost the house. And I was seeing a counsellor and Dad couldn't afford to pay for it any more. Then about the same time, a really close friend of mine died and I'm still really upset about that. And then with Dad's new partner, things have all moved too fast again. Within a couple of months of meeting her, she moved in with her two children and now, a few weeks later, they are about to get married. Mum's better now. And Dad, I want to be happy for him. I'm so happy he's met someone cos he was so unhappy for so long. And I really like my new sisters. But it's just been so fast.

Tom (16):

My school expelled me after my GCSE's, for bad health management. No one understands about diabetes at that school. Basically I had one hypo and I dislocated my shoulder and they got scared. They have training courses on everything else from like asthma to epilepsy, to ADHD, everything basically, except for diabetes. Which, personally, I think is very important because there are 1.2 million of us plus the million that haven't been diagnosed. In my opinion it's the grimmest thing you can have. But the thing is you just don't have the sort of - I don't know if energy is the right word - when you're 16. I mean, I know an awful lot of people with diabetes and at this age, you just don't want to do the blood tests and record the results. I can't get myself out of the cycle. It's like a big habit not to do it, because you'd just rather be enjoying yourself.

Emma (14):

Well, we've not really had any problems at home. I was upset when mum and dad split up when I was four. At first, we had to move into a hideous flat, then we got a little terraced house. Mum had a relationship for a long time which didn't work out. Then she met Phil and they had Tom together. Then they split up and he moved out (laughs). Then it turned out our next door neighbour had a brother who is now our stepdad. We moved into this house and then they had Amy. So I've gained another dad, lots of brothers and sisters and mum and dad get on fine. I do have very close friends. Some are at my church which I love. I go there with mum and my brothers. If I've needed to talk to someone, I talk to mum. We've talked a lot recently about GCSE options. She got me into the school I wanted. She's always been supportive, told us exactly what's going on. We've all just helped each other along.

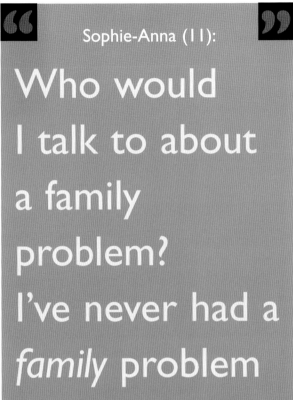

Sophie-Anna (11):

Who would I talk to about a family problem? I've never had a *family* problem

Chapter 6 The people who help us

Ronaldo (age 9):

My granddad's 64, grandma's 61. They've looked after me since I was small. If one of them died I'd feel really bad. I'm able to talk with them about stuff.

Fred (14):

There are some days when I see my friends more than I see my family.

Frances (16):

It's helpful to have a friend to talk to. You can whinge about parents (laughing).

Kevin (11):

Me and my friend Tom do this thing at school where you sit in places. There are three places and we call each one a thinking spot. We either sit on this wall, or sit on these steps, or sit on this step up. And when we sit there, we talk about stuff. Like he told me who his best friend was. We told each other secrets and stuff. I haven't said yet about mum and dad being divorced, not yet. And Emily, she's the one who's most my friend out of the girls I like. The others are not really too special to me but she's nice to me and stuff.

Hector (13):

I maybe talk to my girlfriend about family stuff but no-one else really. She's got parents who have split up as well. I talked to her about mum's new partner. I don't really talk to my friends Matt and Steve. They're important to me, but I probably wouldn't talk to either of them about that sort of stuff. Because it's usually girls who talk about this kind of stuff. We wouldn't do that. Well we might do when we are older. Not now.

Jack (13):

I've known Jet all my life since I was like a week old. I see him every day at school. He's in my class. I can talk easily to both mum and dad but I can talk to Jet about anything. Jet and me and the rest of them, there's like a group of us who are all friends. Maybe some boys don't talk about this stuff, but I do. I'm won't lose contact with Jet, definitely not.

Elizabeth (12):

My aunt is quite funny, kind of strange. Sometimes she is quite bossy and she says all this funny stuff to her husband Jim. But I think Jim just puts up with it because they both love each other. They just say this stuff to each other and put up with each other.

Cathy (15):

Deborah is my auntie, my mum's sister. John's her husband. They're absolutely fantastic. They're like surrogate parents to us. The one thing my auntie said to me was 'If you think of your life as a sink, some people are drains and they drain your life. But some people are taps and they fill your life'. And they've always said that me and my sister are their taps (laughing). And when I was born, they bought me this little rainbow crystal and said that I light up their lives. And they understand that living with my step-dad sometimes gets too much for me. And they've always said that if ever I need a break, I can just pack my bags and go over there straight away. Just as long as Mum's fine with it.

Quentin (17):

I would mostly go talk to my auntie for a problem. She's a social worker and she is like 'Mrs Understanding' about everything. I think I told her first when I started smoking. But I'm very close to grandma too. She's really cool, mad in the head, losing it in her old age. I remember in a restaurant she suddenly said to me 'You drink, you smoke, you bite your nails, you're a disgrace'. She's really, really loving. She knows I love her. I see her every day. And Uncle Matt, my mum's brother is like a big brother or a dad sort of figure. He has been ever since my grandpa died. We always used to be together. But Uncle Matt has three girls and he is a 'bloke's bloke', into his rugby and football. And because me and Pele haven't really had a dad all the time, we like fight with him, watch the football with him. I don't think I would ever tell him that I loved him, but…(laughs).

Pele (14):

I talk to my auntie. I can just talk to her about stuff. And then there's her husband and their three daughters. They're all like between twenty and thirty so they're just like older people. I see them all every week. I just, like, look up to them and stuff.

Callum (8):

There's my friend Sam and my cousin Sam who is better, a lot more important. And my cousin Sam is younger. He is only nearly eight. He is probably the best friend I have ever had. Janine is Sam's mum. She's my aunt, my mum's sister. She is great. She always plays a game with me and it's really funny. Because my mum is not very playful when she is not on holiday because she always has work to do.

Rob (12):

If I had a problem, I think my teacher would be the first person I'd go to. Cos I wouldn't exactly like go to my dad and say 'Me, mum and my stepdad have been having an argument'. I'd prefer to go to my teacher, because I know my teacher wouldn't say anything.

Gabriella (8):

My mum's dad is really fun. Whenever I come to his house he lets us play hairdressers with his hair. He has quite short hair and it's all white. I really like it. It's silky and he never has any knots in. So he lets us get a comb and then we always play hairdressers and say 'What style do you want?' We like doing Elvis Presley.

Frances (16):

It's helpful to have a friend to talk to. You can whinge about parents (laughing). I've talked a lot to my next door neighbour. When dad's new partner first moved in, I started to see less of my dad and I didn't like it. It had been just me and Leanne and then there were like lots of us. And though I feel mean saying it, I feel it was kind of her fault. I remember writing in my diary that I liked her a lot but it was difficult because she was taking attention away from me. It seems very selfish of me. So I went to my neighbour about that. That was helpful. She gave me some advice, sort of saying 'Well, he is going to be happy now. You should let him be happy' and stuff like that.

Louise (12):

My head of year is nice. If I had a problem, I'd talk to her. But I wouldn't want to be without my best friend. No, I'll always have one of them.

Robert (9):

Down the road there is a second hand shop with all sorts of stuff. The woman who owns it is Sheena and I'm friends with her. I'm her best customer. I'm always in there. I bought her a birthday present and at times she buys me one. Every Saturday when I get pocket money I go down there to look. I quite like it because we're friends and she's quite close to me. And one thing is - but I don't think it's got anything to do with our friendship - is that she lowers the prices for me. It's hard to know exactly how old she is but she is a grown up.

Rory (11):

I love having so many brothers and sisters because of mum and dad being divorced. Jamie's five years younger than me but I still get on with him. It helps a lot in this street because there are no children my age. I'm in the middle because my sister Kim is older than me but everyone else is younger. So I can look up and ask advice from Kim and then I like it when Jamie looks up and asks advice from me.

 Sonya (age 13):

My stepsister is more of a best friend but also a sister. She's my very best friend because she's my sister.

Sabrina (17):

You can't meet a nicer man than Grandpa. He's just like the BFG. He's lovely, interested in everything I do. He's been more of a dad to me than my dad has. He used to take us all to school in a morning. And because it were all a bit dodgy at home after mum and dad split up, me and grandpa used to eat porridge together. And he always used to say 'It's not too hot, it's not too cold, it's just right'. And he used to say it every morning. We both used to say it to each other. They stick in your memory those things. He used to make the porridge just perfect every morning. He'd never rush it. Mum used to be like 'Come on, come on, you'll be late for school'. And Grandpa would say, 'She can't go yet, it's got to be just right'. If anything happened to him or grandma, it would be like a parent died. I see them all the time.

Paul (11):

Finn's my schoolmate, best mate. I've known him since I started school. He plays a lot with me and he helps me when I'm down. He helps the most when I'm down. Like if my mum shouted at me and I felt that she didn't love me any more. And same with my dad.

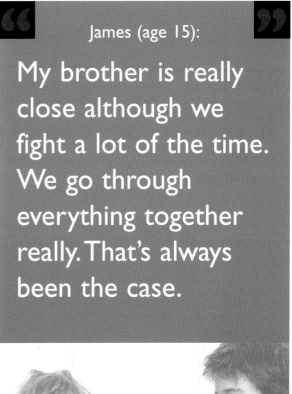

"
James (age 15):

My brother is really close although we fight a lot of the time. We go through everything together really. That's always been the case.

Nina (15):

I talk to my friend's mum quite a bit. I can talk to her about anything really. It's a bit different from talking to your mum because I can sort of tell her about stuff I probably wouldn't tell my mum about, like stuff that I've done.

Joey (18):

There was one teacher who was my favourite ever teacher sort of thing. I got on with her very well and I spoke to her a bit because I went through times, obviously, when I was kind of getting down about mum and dad. And if I was down in her lesson or something, she would notice. She'd take me outside and say, 'Well look you can talk to me about it', sort of thing. So I'd tell her about it a bit. But I mean, if I wanted to talk seriously about stuff, it would probably be immediate family, mum or dad or sometimes my brothers as well, particularly Alex. He's five years older than me. I talk to him because he's almost like, not like a father figure, but he gives me advice and stuff. But he's also someone more on my wavelength.

Fred (14):

I skateboard with all my friends now. It started off with just one person and then everyone got their skateboards and now we all go. There's my brother's friends, there's year nines and year tens and year elevens, who all skateboard together in a big group. Sometimes there's sort of twenty odd and like there are some days when I see my friends more than I see my family and stuff.

Robert (9):

Lottie's my best friend at the moment. She understands me, I understand her. We've been friends ever since mum and her mum became friends, quite a while. She is at my school in the same year as me. I think she's a bit older than me. She might be ten. I haven't seen many boys who are friends with girls because you know girls play with girls and do girls stuff and boys play with boys doing football stuff. She comes round 24/7, virtually every day because she's a good friend. Her parents say yes. We do cooking here or play games at dad's.

 ### Sophia (13):

Well I understand more now about parents splitting up and why they do it because I fell out seriously with one of my friends. In year five and six, we were really good friends. But we fell out in year seven and eight. We constantly fell out and some of them were really bad fall outs. Things got a bit nasty. But we've both grown up now and we realise that we still want to be really good friends. And we still are. It's made it stronger.

Jake (age 14):

Providing parents act properly, divorce shouldn't be a problem.

Hetti (14):

You're not affected by your parents in everything. I mean you've got to have it within yourself to get on in the first place.

Kevin (11):

Whenever like you get a wish bone and I get the right end, I always wish that they would get back together and wouldn't argue very much. But because I've wished that for years and years and years but it hasn't come true, sometimes now, I sometimes wish that I could fly.

Louise (17):

I never wanted my dad and mum to split up so I was like, there was always that jealousy there, with their new partners. I was like you can't have my dad, you can't have my mum. You live in a dream world that they are getting back together. But I don't believe that now. My mum's like, she's had her two kids, she's happy where she is. She has been with him for like eight years now.

Callum (8):

I sometimes want them to be in the same house but then I think that a row would probably break out – cos there'd only be one computer and that would be disastrous. So it is better as it is.

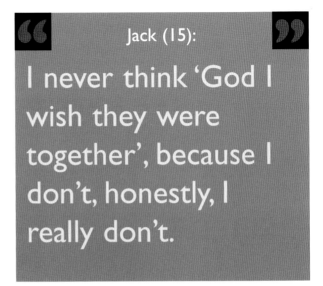

Jack (15):

I never think 'God I wish they were together', because I don't, honestly, I really don't.

Sabrina (17):

I never wanted them to get back together when they split up and I knew it was always for the best. I could tell that from when I was six or whatever.

Becky (16):

Mum and Dad have both gone their separate ways and they seem happier, so let them be. But it has been hectic. It's like, been moved from house to house and school to school. Ain't really been settled. After the divorce we ain't really been settled. Until now.

Ralph (14):

It was upsetting when mum and dad split up. I wanted them back together but it's fine now. I'm OK about it now cos like I'm older and I understand it better. So yeah, I think you forget about it, all your emotions go.

Cathy (15):

One thing I've noticed is my friends, if they've got a problem, they seem less able to cope with it than I am really. It's just little things, like when I went on the school trip. Some people, they've never been away from their parents for more than a day. And within a day, they were crying and wanting to go home. I'm used to being away from my parents like for a week at a time. So I was absolutely fine. I think that's one of the positive things about divorce. It does make you stronger and more independent. At the same time, I know for a fact that I would have reacted differently if they'd divorced now rather than when I was 7. Because I'm much more my own person and have my own opinion now. I've accepted it, but I would be much happier if they were together and happy. It sounds weird, but I think because I was only 7, I just accepted it. Whereas now, if I had to go through those initial months again, it would be really hard.

Nina (15):

Like, when they split up, I wasn't really upset with those things because I thought it was for the best and everything. Probably just 'cos I'm older now, I understand more about it. That stuff's not the most important thing in my life. But I still think it was for the best. Definitely. I just thought it was much unhappier with them living together. I just thought that if it was better for mum, it would make it better for us. It didn't affect me much really because I didn't really see dad that much even when we were living together. There's a good atmosphere now and everyone like gets on well. And the three of us, me, my mum and my sister, we can sort of do stuff together. We can go out together and, I don't know, it's just like easy going as well.

Joey (18):

I think the divorce has changed me. I think I'm probably less sort of sheltered if you like. Because it was quite tough when they were going through the divorce and separation and stuff. And I think it has kind of toughened me in a way. I mean, I disagree with researchers who say that whatever, it is divorce that damages children. I am not damaged by, well it depends how you define damaged, damaged in terms of yes, it hurt and it was hard at the time. But I've got used to it now and it's not something that I'm permanently 'ohhh' about. And it has affected me, I'm sure it has. But it's not like I suddenly changed when they got divorced. But I'm sure I'd have a different outlook on bits of life if my parents had stayed together all my life. And I know that. But I'm not damaged by it, definitely not. I think I'm less naive about relationships because I don't take them for granted.

Sabrina (17):

It made me a lot wiser cos of my mum and dad. You're more sort of like looking out for yourself, even with boyfriends. Like I've been out with them, and it's like 'Don't mess me around'. I feel stronger now. I am a stronger person inside. If I've got something to say I'll say it. I won't be the sort of person who will just sit there and let somebody do something to me.

Bobby (12):

Well I can't exactly remember, I was four or three when they divorced. But I think I was feeling a bit down and like 'this shouldn't have happened' and I felt like I needed to be the man of the house. It's been a bit busy but now I feel that it has kind of changed my life in a better, rather than a worse way. Most of my friends have got parents who have split up. We don't really think about it. If a friend said, 'I'm feeling sad', then we would talk about it and just have a big conversation. Because my friends are quite like me and we just talk about stuff. But if someone's parents split up, then now it's not such a big deal because it happens all the time. And so, well (long pause)…we don't kind of find those things very interesting.

Rachel (20):

I often think about it all. A lot of the opinions I have about it are probably formed. So I am trying to think about it openly as well, trying to make sure that, you know, what I do think about it is correct. If you are rigid then you break. If you are bendable then you can carry on. I think I go through a cycle in how I feel about how it. Obviously, what happens to you makes you the way you are. So if you change things, you don't know what kind of person you would be. And I think I'm not too bad a person. I suppose you don't always want to take responsibility for the ways things are, and if there is something to blame, like divorce, it makes it easier. But it is not always that simple. I think all parents pass on neuroses to their children, even the normal ones. So I think possibly I might be more a product of the way my actual parents are, rather than because they are divorced.

Jake (14):

I have to say I didn't have feelings about the divorce then and I don't now. As far as I can see, the divorce hasn't been a big problem to me. Providing parents act properly, divorce shouldn't be a problem. I mean I don't want to criticise what you're doing, but there's a lot of fuss nowadays about talking about things. And I think that in some ways, for younger people, talking about things can just make them worse. Because I think a lot of people can just sort of deal with things providing they're not going over and over them. I think if you're like suicidally depressed, or compulsively cutting yourself, then it is a good thing, obviously. But I think in a lot of instances it's just best to let go. The going over of what are really everyday problems, problems that affect millions of people, is not something appropriate for everyone. Is it a third or two thirds of marriages that end in divorce? So you can't say it's something shocking. I suppose I think it's strange to be singling people out to talk about this. It's interesting in a way, because you wouldn't say all this in an ordinary conversation. It's not awkward for me but I do feel it's unnecessary, unnecessary for me. But if it helps someone else, that's fine.

Hector (13):

I sometimes wanted a dad but I've never like wanted them to get back together. It's been fine, it's been good. A nice life so far. No massively huge problems. Normal is how I would see it probably. Well, just because you split up, it doesn't mean that you are going to ruin your children's lives. Because it didn't ruin mine.

Jason (16):

Well the divorce was a long time ago. And all that was just boring. Just them two fighting over who had a grandfather clock. When they separated for the first time I was really upset, but then I was left with my dad for quite a while and could realise why my mum had left. I don't know, all that with mum and dad, it's just not worth my time. I mean I've got much more important things that I'd much rather be doing, like enjoying myself, *moving on.*

Chapter 8

Jack (age 15):

A stable marriage and some children

Clare (14):

To settle down, get a good job and be happy.

Joey (18):

To remain close to my family whatever happens, to stay close to all of them.

Louise (17):

One thing I've always known, I've never, ever wanted to be, like, with no job opportunities. To be like thirty years old with no qualifications, no life going for me. I've never wanted that. I've always wanted, by the time I'm thirty, to have like my big house.

Clare (14):

I'd like to just settle down, get a good job and be happy really. And like I'd hate it if I fell out with my parents at some stage and stopped talking. I mean, I've heard of people that have fallen out with their parents and stopped talking for years. And sort of not kept in contact and then just turned cold on each other. But who've they got to turn to? Like they have their partner, but then stuff gets bad with their partner, and then your whole life just goes down the drain. Cos you have trouble at work, you have trouble at home and there's nothing you can do about it. It's really important to keep that bond.

Tom (16):

I want to be a nurse. I don't want to be a doctor because they're not at all 'hands on'. Whereas a nurse is there the whole time making sure that everything goes all right. I want to specialise in paediatrics or be a community nurse.

Archie (12):

Mum and her partner don't have children. Although we might be having a baby. We're not sure yet. I'd prefer it. I want a baby brother or sister. I wouldn't mind which, I just want a baby brother or sister. Well, we were doing it in PSE. We were asked 'What would you like for the future?' and I put down, I said a baby brother or sister. And the teacher goes 'But you've got to think about the consequences' and she said 'What if it's crying all night?' and I said, 'Well, it's worth it'.

Karen (15):

I personally would like to have it that everything and everyone stays together. It is quite funny actually. I believe in true love you see (laughing). So that's why I think it is a bit sad really when it is not working out. And it seems a bit strange that it has happened so often actually. I don't understand why it should be happening.

Bobby (12):

I'd like to have Tom, my stepbrother, living with me more. And I'd like a family and children because they're so enthusiastic and stuff. And maybe not as, maybe not as weird and complex as my family has got now. A bit less busy, a bit less hibbly cobbly.

Don (9):

I'd like a cat. And to get a few of my friends from my old school back because I miss them a bit. And if I did split up with a partner, then we could live quite close to each other instead of moving somewhere else.

Chaz (14):

I would get more dogs. We used to have loads of pets at one time.

Fred (14):

Something to do with music things. But also being able to see my family any time. But I'm not sure. The thing is with this band, if it was successful, there would be a lot of touring and things. And I'm not sure I'd see as much as maybe I'd want to see the family.

James (15):

That I end up having a sort of, a stable marriage, if I ever do have one. And have some children, maybe one or two. I mean if I do marry someone and have children and then I get divorced, I mean I don't really want to do that to my children. Because it is a pain really having to go from house to house. To have children and stay married, I'd much rather it was that way round.

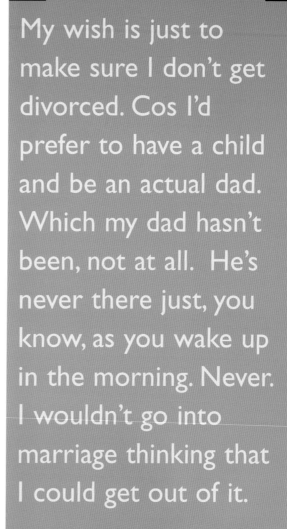

Pele (14):

My wish is just to make sure I don't get divorced. Cos I'd prefer to have a child and be an actual dad. Which my dad hasn't been, not at all. He's never there just, you know, as you wake up in the morning. Never. I wouldn't go into marriage thinking that I could get out of it.

Acknowledgments

In 2001-2002 we followed up 60 of the young people who took part in our previous project out of which Parent Problems! was produced. In this second book, we have put together their views on what has been happening in their lives since that time.

Our greatest debt is to the 60 young people who agreed to take part in our second study. They generously agreed to talk to us when all of them had more pressing claims on their time. They taught us much about family life, but also about many other dimensions of their experience. In particular, they taught us that parental divorce is only one of many possible challenges in a young person's life and that we, as researchers, should be mindful of that. To all of them, a big thank you.

We would also like to thank the Economic and Social Research Council for funding this research and for contributing to the costs of producing this book. We are especially grateful to Adrienne Katz, our publisher at Young Voice, whose enthusiasm and commitment has once again helped us through the publishing process.
The research was carried out at the Centre for Research on Family, Kinship & Childhood at the University of Leeds. Thank you to our colleagues there, Carol Smart and Amanda Wade, for their encouragement and support.

Bren Neale and Jen Flowerdew

E·S·R·C
ECONOMIC
& SOCIAL
RESEARCH
COUNCIL

Centre for Research on Family, Kinship & Childhood,
Department of Sociology and Social Policy,
University of Leeds.